Computer Science, Technology and

INTUITION AND COMPUTER
PROGRAMMING (WT)

COMPUTER SCIENCE, TECHNOLOGY AND APPLICATIONS

Peer-to-Peer Storage: Security and Protocols
Nouha Oualha and Yves Roudier (Authors)
2010. 978-1-61668-199-9

Persuasion On-Line and Communicability: The Destruction of Credibility in the Virtual Community and Cognitive Models
Francisco V. Cipolla-Ficarra (Author)
2010. 978-1-61668-268-2

Intuition and Computer Programming (WT)
Michael Weigend (Author)
2010. 978-1-61668-330-6

Peer-to-Peer Storage: Security and Protocols
Nouha Oualha and Yves Roudier (Authors)
2010. 978-1-61668-462-4

Relational Databases and Open Source Software Developments
Jennifer R. Taylor (Editor)
2010. 978-1-61668-468-6

Semantic Web: Standards, Tools and Ontologies
Kimberly A. Haffner (Editor)
2010. 978-1-61668-471-6

Logic of Analog and Digital Machines
Paolo Rocchi (Author)
2010. 978-1-61668-481-5

Design and Performance of Biometric System
John T. Elsworth (Editor)
2010. 978-1-61668-524-9

Semantic Web: Standards, Tools and Ontologies
Kimberly A. Haffner (Editor)
2010. 978-1-61668-540-9

Logic of Analog and Digital Machines
Paolo Rocchi (Author)
2010. 978-1-61668-481-5

Design and Performance of Biometric System
John T. Elsworth (Editor)
2010. 978-1-61668-524-9

Semantic Web: Standards, Tools and Ontologies
Kimberly A. Haffner (Editor)
2010. 978-1-61668-540-9

Persuasion On-Line and Communicability:
The Destruction of Credibility in the Virtual
Community and Cognitive Models
Francisco V. Cipolla-Ficarra (Author)
2010. 978-1-61668-701-4

Intuition and Computer Programming (WT)
Michael Weigend (Author)
2010. 978-1-61668-813-4

Logic of Analog and Digital Machines
Paolo Rocchi (Author)
2010. 978-1-61668-815-8

Computer Science, Technology and Applications

INTUITION AND COMPUTER PROGRAMMING (WT)

MICHAEL WEIGEND

Nova Science Publishers, Inc.
New York

NOTICE TO THE READER

The Publisher has taken reasonable care in the preparation of this book, but makes no expressed or implied warranty of any kind and assumes no responsibility for any errors or omissions. No liability is assumed for incidental or consequential damages in connection with or arising out of information contained in this book. The Publisher shall not be liable for any special, consequential, or exemplary damages resulting, in whole or in part, from the readers' use of, or reliance upon, this material.

Independent verification should be sought for any data, advice or recommendations contained in this book. In addition, no responsibility is assumed by the publisher for any injury and/or damage to persons or property arising from any methods, products, instructions, ideas or otherwise contained in this publication.

This publication is designed to provide accurate and authoritative information with regard to the subject matter covered herein. It is sold with the clear understanding that the Publisher is not engaged in rendering legal or any other professional services. If legal or any other expert assistance is required, the services of a competent person should be sought. FROM A DECLARATION OF PARTICIPANTS JOINTLY ADOPTED BY A COMMITTEE OF THE AMERICAN BAR ASSOCIATION AND A COMMITTEE OF PUBLISHERS.

LIBRARY OF CONGRESS CATALOGING-IN-PUBLICATION DATA

Available upon Request
ISBN: 978-1-61668-330-6

Published by Nova Science Publishers, Inc. ⏎ New York

CONTENTS

PREFACE

Intuitive models are self-evident, holistic mental concepts about the world. They are based upon experience in many domains and people are certain and confident to understand them completely. Programmers use them, when they try to understand the semantics of a computer program, explain an algorithmic idea to someone else, check the logical correctness of existing code or create new computer programs. This book focuses on intuitive models (declarative knowledge) applied by programming novices concerning state transitions versus data processing, allocation of activity within a running program, and the assignment of names to entities and function calls.

1. INTRODUCTION

Intuitive models are self-evident, holistic (Gestalt-like) mental concepts about the world (Fischbein 1987, diSessa 2001). They are based upon experience in many domains and people are certain and confident to understand them completely. Programmers use them, when they try to understand the semantics of a computer program, explain an algorithmic idea to someone else, check the logical correctness of existing code or create new computer programs.

A typical example in the field of computer programming is the container model. We can imagine that during the run of a computer program information is stored in containers or taken from containers. This concept is intuitive, because we are very familiar with containers. We have learned (by experience in early childhood) that a thing we have put into a container remains there until someone removes it. And when we search for a match we look for a box containing matches.

In cognitive psychology sometimes a distinction is made between declarative and procedural knowledge (Anderson 2004; Haberlandt 1994). Intuitive models like the container analogy are declarative knowledge about the world ("knowing that"). But there is also intuitive procedural knowledge ("knowing how") like riding a bike, bipedal walking or sorting a deck of cards. A procedural intuition is a task a person can effectively solve but cannot necessarily tell how she or he made it. That does not imply that the subject doesn't use an algorithm. But eventually the algorithm is not conscious or the person is not able to represent it and therefore cannot explicate and communicate it. Still there is the subjective certainty (a characteristic property of intuition) to be able to solve the task.

Some intuitive models have been cultivated and formalized by computer scientists. Abstract data types and standard classes in object oriented programming languages combine data structures with certain operations to coherent chunks of knowledge. For instance, the structure of a stack of plates already implies that immediate access is only possible by putting another plate on top (push-operation) or taking away the top plate (pop-operation).

Software patterns like the iterator pattern describe algorithmic ideas on a high level. Professional agile software development (Extreme Programming) starts with a "project metaphor", which comprises the architecture of a complex system in one coherent concept.

Intuitive models can be seen (from a psychological perspective) as internal cognitive concepts. But they are also (inter-subjective) cultural phenomena. In order to communicate them (in discussions or software documentations), an individual person has to externalize and represent them within the material world using metaphors (transferring knowledge from one domain to another), encodings (verbal language, static pictures, movies) and examples.

Illustrations and explanations in text books, software documentations (which have to be understood by a heterogeneous audience) and educational debuggers (like Jeliot) visualizing program runs are based upon explicated intuitive models.

This article focuses on intuitive models (declarative knowledge) applied by programming novices concerning the following issues: State transitions versus data processing, allocation of activity within a running program, assignment of names to entities and function calls. Evidence is collected from visualisation exercises, workshops using game-like software applications and pencil and paper-games. These workshops took place mostly in high schools and primary schools in the years 2005 – 2009.

2. HOW CAN I PUT IT?
REPRESENTATION OF INTUITIVE MODELS

When you tell someone about your intuition or try to write it down, you have to externalize an internal mental concept. You create a physically existent and perceivable representation.

An intuitive model is a persistent cognitive phenomenon. However, its representations might vary and might be volatile. Obviously, for one intuitive model there exists an infinite diversity of possible representations. Imagine a programmer - let us call her Sarah -, who is explaining an algorithmic idea to someone else scribbling a sketch on a piece of paper. First she keeps it very simple. When she realizes that her communication partner does not understand, she adds more visual details and verbal information. She even might create new representations ad hoc during the communication process, designing them according to the addressee's assumed knowledge. Some of these pictures or verbal phrases explicating the intuitive model are used just once and never again. They may be forgotten after a short time. But the intuitive concept itself is persistent. However, the distinction between the model and its representation is analytical and sometimes language use blurs the difference. Is a certain picture an intuitive model or is it one out of many representations of an intuitive model? I distinguish three dimensions of explicating an intuitive model:

- Encoding. An intuitive model can be explicated using different expressive means like words, static images or movies. In a concrete communication situation several encoding techniques may be combined.

- Metaphors. The representation of an intuitive model has to be within a domain of familiar knowledge to be easily understood. The transfer of knowledge from a (familiar) source domain to a (not that familiar) target domain is called metaphor.
- Exemplification. A representation of an abstract intuitive model is a concrete example out of a variety of possible representations.

2.1. ENCODING AND MEMORY

Paivio's theory of dual encoding states that knowledge is stored in memory verbally and imaginally (Paivio 1971; 1986). Examples of imaginal knowledge representations are pictures, drawings, maps and diagrams. Verbal representations are based upon a symbolic system (language) and include text phrases and mathematical models. It has been shown that a simple and easily to describe image (e.g. a house) after having seen it only once can be remembered better than a written word. Paivio explains this fact by assuming that pictures are stored in two ways: in an analog way as purely visual content and additionally in a symbolic (digital) way as a word or phrase describing its meaning. Dual encoding increases the chance to remember a piece of knowledge later.

In a problem solving situation chunks of information are processed very quickly and partly in parallel. Recent research in cognitive psychology leads to the assumption that working memory is a central component for information processing (Dehn 2008, Baddeley 1998, 2003). Working memory provides a quick access to relevant information but its capacity is very limited. Thus, intuitive models should be encoded in a way that working memory load is minimal. According to Baddeley's model, working memory contains subcomponents for storing verbal and visual information and a central executive.

Verbal information that can be articulated in speech is stored in the phonological loop. It is analogous to an audio tape recorder loop that is able to store verbal information, which can be articulated in not more than two seconds. This implies that just one complex object reference like "the name of my eldest brother's second daughter's dog" might block the working memory completely and prevent any problem solving. On the other hand short verbal identifiers for relevant objects and operations like in "E equals m c square" are of advantage.

The spatiovisual sketchpad is responsible for storing static visual images and spatial information related to movement and locations. Storage is limited in capacity typically to about three or four objects for a matter of seconds (Baddeley 1996). Simple patterns like blocks displayed in a matrix or symmetrical figures are easier to recall than complex ones (Kemps 1999). This indicates that an animated program visualization should be reduced to a few dynamic elements. Otherwise recipients may not notice when objects move, change color or disappear. Systems that automatically create UML diagrams (e.g. BlueJ) or visualizations of program executions (e.g. Jelliot) often fail to keep their visual output simple. First and foremost this is due to their incapability to abstract and to distinguish between important und unimportant elements of the modeled computer program.

The phonological loops may assist image processing by attaching labels to the shapes involved (Pearson et al. 1999). Thus, visual models of algorithmic ideas should be easier to comprehend when they consist of meaningful elements the recipient is able to recognize and represent verbally.

2.2. METAPHORS

The technical language of computer scientists is full of metaphors. In rhetoric a metaphor is defined as a transfer of meaning (Baumgarten 2005). A phrase from a certain domain of knowledge (target domain) is replaced by a different phrase from another domain (source domain). Examples:

- A variable is a container for data.
- A function is a factory that produces new data.

There are other speech figures similar to metaphors. In a metonym the target phrase is replaced by a different expression from the same domain of knowledge. Example: An array is a row of items.

In a simile the two expressions from different domain are connected using the particle "like", for instance "Instances of a class are like houses which are built according to the same construction plan". Many metaphors in computer science are dead or necessary metaphors. That means that there is no specific expression within the target domain which could be used. For example, programmers say that a function *receives* arguments and *returns* the result. In this case knowledge from the domain of human interaction is transferred to the domain of computer programs. The function is seen as person receiving something from another person and then giving something back. But there is no other way to say it. In many programming languages (Java, Python, ActionScript) the word return is even part of the syntax and is used for this operation.

From the perspective of rhetoric, metaphors are used to make a speech interesting. It is playing with meaning. The suspension is increased, when the source domain is unusual and far away from the target domain. Cognitive linguistics consider metaphors not just as a means to improve speech but – roughly speaking - as a means to improve thinking. Lakoff and Nuñez (1997) describe conceptual metaphors in mathematics. Conceptual metaphors are frequently used in math teaching bridging the gap between familiar ways to think and a new and still unfamiliar domain. For example, the conceptual metaphor "arithmetic is object collection". maps activities and entities from a physical domain to a mathematical domain:

Numbers are collections of physical objects of equal size. An addition is joining two collections to a bigger collection, and so on. There are many suggestions for classroom activities which are based upon this metaphor. Usually students "play" all kinds of arithmetic operations by moving objects on the table.

This example illustrates that the source domain must be intuitive to be of help. Only when a child is certain that the number of objects does not change while rearranging them, the metaphor helps understanding arithmetic. Thus intuitions (certain knowledge) serve as source concepts for conceptual metaphors.

The metaphor "arithmetic is object collection" could be called a structural analogy. When children move beads or nuts on the table discovering arithmetic concepts, this is called analog reasoning. Knowledge from a familiar domain is transferred to another still unfamiliar domain. Analog reasoning plays an important part in the history of science. For example, Galileo used knowledge about the orbit of the moon as basis for his theory that the earth is also moving in space (English 2004).

In general, metaphors need not to be structural analogies of the target concept. Only systems of equal complexity can be truly analog. But especially in the field of computer programming intuitive models often have a different structure than the target. In many cases models are used in order to *reduce* complexity and working memory load. A model that is supposed to explain the idea of an algorithm usually is simpler than the corresponding program. Thus, the development of a computer program on the basis of an intuitive model usually is more than analog reasoning.

I consider metaphorizing as a dimension of knowledge representation. An intuitive model is a piece of knowledge that is more abstract than a metaphor. For one intuition there might exist several metaphors representing it. For example the concept of a variable in a computer program can be understood using a container model (see section 6.3.). Still, "container" is a rather abstract concept and can be visualized using different metaphors:

- Metaphor 1: There is box with a label outside representing the name of the variable. Inside the box there is a thing representing the value. The value can be changed by replacing the thing.
- Metaphor 2: Imagine a blackboard with a title written permanently on the frame (name). In the middle of the blackboard there is some text written with chalk (value). This text can easily be wiped out and replaced by something else.
- Metaphor 3: Imagine a table with one column and a title on top (name), which is separated from values below by a horizontal line. Below the title of the table there is the initial value of the variable. When an assignment name = value takes place, the current value is struck out and the new value is written below.

2.3. EXEMPLIFICATION

Each physically existing representation of an intuitive model is an example out of an infinite diversity of possibilities. Since you can always change a verbal explanation or a picture in some details without changing the meaning substantially, each metaphor is an example. But the are also non-metaphoric examples which are taken from the same domain as the target. In rhetoric they are called metonyms. The example list [1, 2, 3] may be considered as a metonym for a Python list. There are several principles, which might be considered when creating or choosing examples, including simplicity, richness, usability and representiveness

Simplicity. Not every example represents an intuitive model. If it is too complex, it loses its coherent Gestalt. If it is too simple it might just represent a special case (e.g. a list with none or just one element). Nevertheless such oversimplified example might be important within a collection of examples. Examples are often used in reference cards, which cover the essentials of a programming language on very limited space (see table 1).

**Table 1. Excerpt from a reference card for the
programming language Python, published by o'Reilly 2005**

Operation	Comment
()	An empty tuple
t1 = (0,)	A one-item-tuple (not an expression)
t2 = (0, 'Ni', 1.2, 3)	A four-item tuple

- *Richness.* A rich example reflects more facets of an abstract concept than a poor example. Obviously richness is connected to complexity but it is not the same. A rich example might consist of just a few elements but still cover a lot of information which can be deduced while thinking about it.
- *Applicability.* An example may illustrate how to apply the represented concept in a real computer program. For instance a Python list of names like ["Smith", "Johnson", "Meyer"] might be associated to a list of patients waiting at the doctor's. Applicability might be in conflict with richness. From the above example you cannot deduce whether or not a list may contain objects of different types.
- *Representiveness.* Examples can be more or less representative instances of a category. Kahneman and Tversky (1982) asked students to estimate the probability of sequences of numbers that might occur while throwing a dice. They found that regular sequences like (4, 4, 4, 4, 4) were considered to be less probable than sequences containing different numbers like (2, 5, 1, 2, 3). The latter example seems to be more representative for the concept of random numbers.

3. WAYS TO USE INTUITIVE MODELS IN COMPUTER PROGRAMMING

Computer programmers use intuitive models in different contexts and for different reasons. This section focuses on the different roles of intuitions with regard to comprehension (understanding), explaining, problem solving and validation.

3.1. COMPREHENSION

Comprehension takes place, when a programmer reads source code (including comments) and tries to find out how it works or when a novice reads a section in a reference book in order to get an idea of a certain programming technique.

Fischbein calls intuitive concepts related to understanding semantic intuitions (Fischbein 1987, p. 59 ff). For example a container with a label and some content is a semantic intuition for the concept of variables in computer programs.

Text understanding is discussed in philosophical text hermeneutic. Since Heidegger "understanding" is considered not just as a method of knowledge gain but as a fundamental aspect of "being human" (Capurro 1986). A human has the chance to act freely (undetermined) within the world. This freedom or openness is given through the ability to understand. The hermeneutic circle describes the interpreting a text as an (in principle) infinite cyclic process of elaborating text. Interpreting is a process of questioning. The whole meaning of the document is gathered by considering its parts and the meaning of the parts is understood within the context of the whole. Understanding remains preliminary and is questioned again in each passage of the loop (Capurro 1989). In this regard, the hermeneutic concept of understanding is complementary to Fishbein's semantic intuitions. Hermeneutics emphasizes uncertainty of knowledge whereas intuitions are subjectively certain. A second difference is related to persistency. According to Fischbein and diSessa people never get rid of their intuitions. They are a persistent part of the personality and influence thinking during the whole life. In contrast to that, hermeneutics states that a human being can change and develop by questioning and rethinking. A solution of this contradiction between persistency and change might be this: Although you cannot change your intuitions on purpose, you can get aware of them and find ways to use them in an appropriate way. This competence includes the ability to choose consciously from a repertoire of intuitions and to recognize the limits of an intuitive model.

The hermeneutic questioning of a text can be seen as a search for appropriate semantic intuitions modeling the content. But it might be also helpful to explicate and memorize *inappropriate* intuitions. For instance the concept "length of a list" (number of elements) might be better understood when keeping in mind the difference to the length of a physical entity (meters).

Efforts to understand programming concepts may include experiments. You type some code, run it, and check the result in order to find out whether or not you have understood it right. Experiments are a source of "real world experience" accompanied with sensory input, emotion and excitement. It makes a difference whether you just read about the chemical reaction of sodium and water or whether you actually see and hear it, feel the danger and are surprised when something unexpected happens. In the same way programming experiments seem to be important for understanding, even when no significant gain of new information is expected. Computer programming textbooks and other instructional material usually contain small examples of program code illustrating the application of some abstract concept and inspiring the reader to try it out on the computer.

In April 2004 the students of my informatics class at a German comprehensive school (grade 12) had to study a paper about regular expressions. The material contained some example calls of the Python function findall(). This function accepts a regular expression and a string as arguments. It returns a list of all substrings that match the regular expression.

There were four examples. The expected result of each function call was listed in the second line. Here is an example (translated to English):

>>> findall('g.ass',

'There is a glass lying in the grass)

['glass', 'grass']

14 of the 27 students tried out at least one of these examples at the computer, eight tested all four examples. On the screen they saw exactly the same as on the paper, but obviously they wanted to experience the execution of the function calls on a real computer (weigend 2007).

3.2. EXPLAINING

Explaining has a lot to do with comprehension. You can only explain things you have understood. In contrast to understanding, explaining is an act of communication. When you choose appropriate intuitive models for an explanation you must have the knowledge of the addressee in mind.

When you try to understand you aim to a "global view". Search for comprehension is unspecific and egocentric. In the hermeneutic cycle you extend your knowledge horizon in all directions. You want to be prepared for all kinds of situations and you want to understand the concept as a whole.

Explanations usually are specific. When you explain the idea of an algorithm you want your addressee to reach a certain level of understanding. Thus, explaining intuitions focus on aspects that are considered to be important and ignore peripheral details. Explaining is very important in computer programming. Here are some typical contexts, in which explaining (using intuitive models) takes place:

- Project documentations and comments within program texts explain algorithmic ideas.
- Each program written in a high level programming language is a text document made for humans. It contains meaningful names for variables, classes and methods and should be designed in way that it is easy to understand. In short, programming implies explaining.

- When searching a logical error in a program it might be necessary to explain (specifically) why the program does not yield the expected output.

3.2.1. Focussing

Intuitive models differ in their degree of focussing. To illustrate the principle of limited access to attributes in object oriented programming objects are sometimes compared with castles. Inside the castle there are the attributes, protected like a treasure. Around these – like walls – there are methods, which control the access to certain attributes. The castle model is an example of a highly focussed intuition, used to explain a very special aspect of object oriented programming. In contrast, the container model for variables may be useful for a much wider range of explanations. It is less focussing.

Focussing implies reduction of complexity. To be intuitive, an explaining model must be simple. A focussed model is not necessarily the most simple model suitable to explain a certain content. Fig. 1 shows screenshots from four different animations that visualize the execution of the following Python program:

```
s = [1, 5, 4, 3, 2]
for i in s:
    print i*i
```

This program is an example of an iteration over a list of numbers. Each number is multiplied with itself and the result is printed on screen (Weigend 2007 p. 86 ff).

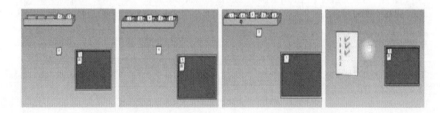

Figure 1. Screenshots from four Flash movies visualizing an iteration (Weigend 2007 p. 87).

In three models the list is visualized by a box with five compartments each containing a card with a number written on it. The calculation of the square is visualized by a flash of white light. The card with the original number is replaced by a new card with the result and this card moves to a blackboard representing the output device.

1. In the first model in each iteration step a card is removed from the box (starting on the left hand side) and then processed.
2. In the second model nothing is removed from the box. Instead, copies of the cards appear one by one and float away in order to be processed.
3. The third model is similar to model 2. The only additional feature is red dot, which is moving from one compartment to the next, indicating the item which is processed in the present step of the iteration.
4. The fourth model deploys a different intuition representing the list. The numbers are written in a column on a sheet. During the iteration all items, which have already been processed are check-marked.

These animations were watched and evaluated by 66 students from computer science classes in Germany and Hong Kong (12 girls, 54 boys, average age 16.6 years). The students had to decide which model they would use to explain the Python program to someone else.

Table 2. Models to explain iteration. Result of a survey with 66 high school students in Hong Kong and Germany

Removing entities (1)	Generating copies (2)	Moving dot (3)	Marking (4)
6 (9%)	13 (20%)	30 (45%)	17 (26%)

Removing items from a collection - like in model 1 - is a very clear and concise intuition for iterations. There is no doubt which item has already been processed. Additionally this model corresponds to many iterations in everyday life, like eating all chocolates from a chocolate box or clearing a dish washer. Although model 1 is the simplest of all presented animations (it has the smallest number of structural components) it was chosen by only 6 students (9%). A possible reason is that removing elements during the iteration implies a change of the list, which does not happen in the program. But this could also be considered to be an unimportant detail, which might be kept in mind additionally.

Most students selected model 3. The advantage of this model might be that it explicates an iterator, an entity that indicates which item of the collection is next. Note that in the program text there is no explicit iterator. (The variable i is just the name of the present item but it is not an iterator.)

A drawback of a focussing model is the risk to be misleading regarding aspects out of the focus. Thus, a focussing intuitive model is a possible source of misconceptions. A way to reduce the risk in explanations is (1) to use many different intuitions each focussing on different aspects and (2) to clarify the scope of application of each intuitive model.

3.3. PROBLEM SOLVING

Computer programming is problem solving. In this section I first present two slightly different roles that intuitive models can play in the context of program creation. Then I discuss two elaborated applications of intuitive models in professional software development: design patterns and use cases.

3.3.1. Anticipatory Intuitions

During a problem solving process, while thinking about possible solutions sometimes people experience a moment of enlightening, a vision how to make it. Fischbein (1987) calls this an anticipatory intuition. In the field of computer programming an anticipatory intuition might be the fundamental idea of an algorithm. Bubblesort for example is based on the idea that in a ascending sorted list of numbers the left neighbour of any number is smaller, if there is a left neighbour. In your mind you focus on just one location within the list. An item is compared with its left neighbour. If this is bigger, both items swap. When this has been done sufficiently often the list is sorted. Although it takes several sentences to describe this idea, it still can be considered as one coherent whole, a Gestalt. This example illustrates that semantic intuition (representing meaning) can support anticipatory intuitions (representing activity). Bubblesort is based on the semantic intuition that in a sorted list the left neighbour is smaller.

In contrast, the anticipatory idea of the straight selection algorithm is supported by the (semantic) intuition of minimum. In a sorted list $[s_0, s_1, ..., s_n]$

each item s_i is the minimum of the sublist $[s_i, s_{i+1}, ..., s_n]$. Thus, a sorted list can easily be constructed be searching for smallest items.

In Extreme Programming (Beck 1999) each project starts with a metaphor, an evocative description of the program architecture. For example, "this program works like a hive of bees, going out for pollen and bringing it back to the hive" is an anticipatory intuitive model for an agent-based information retrieval system (Jeffries 2001).

3.3.2. Paradigmatic Intuitions

Intuitive models can be some kind of pattern how to solve a problem. This is a different role than anticipating a solution. Fischbein (2007) calls such models "paradigmatic intuitions". In the field of computer programming a paradigmatic intuition can be a concrete example representing a whole class of software solutions. It might be a simplified and idealized program text - printed in a "cookbook" - , which can be copied and adapted to fit to a different scenario. A paradigmatic model which can be used for many computer programs is "input – processing – output". A simple interactive program reads data from keyboard, processes them in some way and calculates a result, which is written on screen. The same pattern is used in other contexts:

- A function gets data from its environment via arguments, processes them and returns a result.
- A cgi script (running on a server) gets a querystring or http packet with data, processes them and returns an html page to the remote client.

3.3.3. Intuition and Software Development - Design Patterns

In computer science intuitive models can be found on many levels. On a quite high level of abstraction researchers try to compile structured collections of design patterns (Gamma et al. 1995). A software design pattern is „a solution to a recurring problem in a context". The goal is to make software reusable. It can be considered an intuitive model, which is well elaborated and documented. Patterns must be intuitive to be of worth to software development. Otherwise a programmer would not find an appropriate pattern for her or his problem. A well known design patterns is the iterator pattern. An iterator accesses the items of collection (sequence, set) one by one without exposing the internal structure of the collection. For example in case of a set the iterator guarantees to deliver every element of the collection but the exact order is not predictable since the elements of a set are not in a specific order. Everyday examples of iterators are the medical secretary picking the next patient sitting in the waiting room to be seen by the doctor, or the host of a dinner party introducing all his guests sitting at the table. These examples illustrate that software design patterns are rooted in everyday experience (Riehle & Züllighoven 1995), which must be shared by many people. Cooper points out that in fact, most "patterns are rather discovered than written" (Cooper 2003, p. 6).

3.3.4. Actors in Use Case Diagrams

According to the paradigm of object oriented modeling an industrial software development starts with an object oriented analysis (Balzert 1999). In this phase uses cases are defined, which describe the system functionality. A use case diagram in the Unified Modeling Language (UML) shows which system functions are used by which actor. For example, in a use case diagram modeling the administration of a library actors might be a reader and a clerk. The reader can search for books, borrow and return books. The clerk can put new books into the collection of the library or remove books which are too old. Each actor is an intuitive model of a coherent set of functions (or activities) that belong together. When you define a reasonable system of actors you already have a complete overview of the required system functionality.

3.4. INTUITION AND CHECKING LOGICAL CORRECTNESS

Intuitive models are simple and self-evident, computer programs usually are not. Even small programs, consisting of just a few lines of code might contain errors an experienced programmer does not discover just by reading it. In general, it is not enough just to understand the idea of the program (anticipatory intuition). Still, some detail might be wrong you have not thought about yet. And in some cases even the idea of an algorithm is difficult to gather. Intuitive models can be used to check the correctness of an algorithm which is too complex to be intuitive itself. I call this type of intuitive models (resp. this role) controlling models. They serve as some kind of alarm system ringing when something is wrong. Consider this simple word problem, which is mentioned by Fischbein (1987, p. 40): "0.65 litres of juice cost 2 Dollars. What is the price of 1 litre?" The challenge is to find an appropriate operation to calculate the solution from the given numbers. In this case 2 Dollars must be divided by 0.65 to get the price for 1 l. A useful controlling model might be this: Imagine a small bottle containing 0.65 l and a bigger bottle with 1 l of juice. Obviously the bigger bottle must be more expensive. This model is simpler than a model for the complete solution. It enables you to check certain properties of the result (price per litre must be greater than 2 Dollars), but it does not really prove logical correctness. However, the subjective certainty that an algorithm is correct grows, when it has been checked many times applying different intuitive models.

A software developer uses controlling models when searching for logical errors (debugging) or when inserting assertions into a program. These are invariant conditions which must be true, if the program is correct. The programming language Python provides a simple feature for processing assertions, which is called assert statement. It consists of the key word assert, which is followed by a Boolean expression (condition). During runtime the condition is evaluated. When it is true, nothing happens. When it is false, the interpreter raises an exception. On the screen you see error message, which you can use to localize the error.

Imagine a function that is supposed to sort a list. At the end of the program one could insert an assert statement like this

```
assert len(sorted_list) == len(unsorted_list)
```

The meaning is: The sorted list must have the same length (number of elements) as the original unsorted list. This condition is part of the concept of "sorting". You never lose objects while sorting them. This is self evident. Everybody would accept this without further explanation. This assertion bases upon an intuitive model that does not represent the whole idea of a sorting algorithm (like an anticipatory intuition) but just one aspect of it: "sorting is some kind of rearranging things".

The following listing shows a Python implementation of the very efficient Quicksort algorithm, which was invented by Hoare. It is a recursive function called qsort(), which takes an unsorted list s as input and returns an sorted list with the same items as s. The program includes six assertions. The algorithm as a whole is very difficult to understand. But the assertions are intuitive.

```
def qsort (s):
  s0 = s[:]                # s0 is a copy of s
  if s0 == []:
    return s0
  else:
    assert len(s0) >= 1      #1
  x = s0[0]
  s0.remove(x)
  s1 = []
  s2 = []
  for i in s0:
    if i <= x: s1.append(i)
    else: s2.append(i)
  assert len(s1) < len(s)          #2
  assert len(s1) <= len(s0)        #3
  result = qsort(s1) + [x] + qsort (s2)
  assert len(result) == len(s)     #4
  assert result[0] == min(s)       #5
  assert result[0] <= result[-1]   #6
  return result
```

The assert statements base upon the following intuitions:

#1: The list, which is processed in the following section, must have at least one item.

#2: In the preceding program lines two smaller lists s1 and s2 were created. The list s1 must be shorter than the original list s, since it is used as argument in an recursive call of qsort() in the next program line. Otherwise we would have an infinite recursion and the execution of the function would never stop. (Obiously the same is true for list s2, but this is not considered here.) This reflects a basic property of recursive algorithms: In a recursive call the algorithm is applied to a smaller part of the original problem (here: list).

#3: This is just a variant of #2 using a different Boolean expression.

The next three statements test the postcondition of the function.

#4: Sorting does not change the number of items (see above).

#5: In an ascending sorted list of numbers the first number must be the smallest.

#6: In an ascending sorted list of numbers the first number must be smaller or equal to the last number.

In 2004 a group of 21 students, who were familiar with the Quicksort algorithm and with Python programming, got this program listing without the assert statements and a separate list of appropriate and inappropriate assert statements. The program listing included empty lines at positions where assert statements could be added. The task was to add as many assert statements as possible to the code in order to install an "alarm system" for possible errors. Table 3 shows the results.

A quite interesting observation is that the very simple condition len(result) == len (s) was chosen by only 8 out of 21 students. On the other hand 20 students checked whether the first element of the result list is the smallest. And all students were able to use at least one Boolean expression containing a call of len() in a proper way. This indicates that everybody has understood the concept of assert statements and the usage of the function len(). So, why did many students not get the idea to check the length of the computed list? A possible explanation is that they just were not aware of the concept "sorting is rearranging". When you sort things in everyday life (like stones of different size) you move them without thinking about the informatics implications. You just take it for granted that things do not disappear or are duplicated accidently. But this is only true in a physical environment. A computer program processing data works completely different. A programmer must be aware of this. Thus, finding controlling models implies a careful analysis of intuitions. It means to explicate implicit aspects of algorithms you usually never think about.

Table 3. Frequency of selected assert statements for a sorting program (quicksort) in a test written by 21 students of a computer science class (grade 13) at a German comprehensive school (Weigend 2007)

Assert statement	Frequency
assert len(s) >= 1	21
assert len(s1) < len(s)	7
assert len(s1) <= len(s)	8
assert len(result) == len (s)	8
assert result [0] == min(s)	20
assert result[0] <= result[-1]	8

4. DATA MODELS

Computer programs process data. In this section I discuss two different intuitions representing data: data entities and states.

In many cases people think of variables as containers for data. Using this intuition a statement like x = 1000 is interpreted as "The variable x gets the value 1000" or "1000 is stored in the variable x". These and other phrases like "data input" or "data transport" assume that data are quasi-material entities that can be moved and stored in containers.

By contrast, a state is an immaterial concept. A state might be a meaningful Gestalt associated to some activity and a few other states, which can directly be reached. To *be* sick is something different than to *have* a body temperature of 39°C and headache. When you are sick, you are supposed not to work, but stay at home, consult the doctor and take some medication. Typical connected states are "healthy" or "dead". Such meaningful states are usually identified by significant names. A process can be in states like "sleeping" or "active". But for the state of a running program after the execution of an assignment like x = 1234 there exists no specific word.

In his last major work Erich Fromm (1976) uses the antithetical concepts "to have" and "to be" to discuss two fundamental human orientations – so called modes of existence. The having mode, which predominates in modern societies, roots in the biological urge for survival. Humans are predisposed to collect and possess things. On the other hand human nature includes the desire to *be* a genuine subject – regardless of property –, expressed in sharing, giving and cooperating with others.

4.1. STATES VERSUS DATA ENTITIES

Figure 2 presents screenshots of three animations, which visualize the execution of the following two assignments (Python):

a = 3
b = a

In the first model the value is represented by a data-entity, a card with the number 3 written on it. During the execution of the first statement a box labeled with "a" appears and the card is put into it. Then a copy of this card emerges and moves into a second box.

The second and third model visualize the number 3 by an immaterial state of an object: the position of a disc with numbers, or the position of pearls on a horizontal wire.

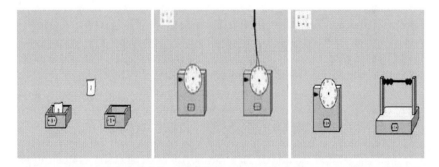

Figure 2. Data and state-oriented visualizations of an assignment (Weigend 2007).

154 high school students from Germany and Hong Kong (average age 17 years, 34 female, 120 male) saw these movies (among others) and had to decide for each, whether it is an appropriate model or not. 133 (86%) of them accepted the first model with moving data entities, but only 100 (65%) the second and 103 (67%) the third (Weigend 2007). The difference between entity- and state-related models is significant. A problem of the state-oriented model in this context is, that it does not visualize the transport of information from a source to a target, which is an important facet of the meaning of the second assignment b = a. Since they are immaterial, states cannot be copied. The concept of copying relates to the generation of a new entity which is identical to an already existing entity.

4.2. MEANINGFUL STATES AND FINITE AUTOMATA

A system consisting of a limited number of states, state transitions and (eventually) activities is called finite state automaton. In theoretical computer science finite state automatons (acceptors) are used to define formal languages. Software developers use automatons to describe the behaviour of computer programs or individual objects within an object oriented system. Finite state automatons are visualized by state transition diagrams. They consist of circles, representing states, and arrows representing state transitions triggered by events (called input) that are described by annotations. When an input triggers some activity, this is annotated behind the input separated by a slash.

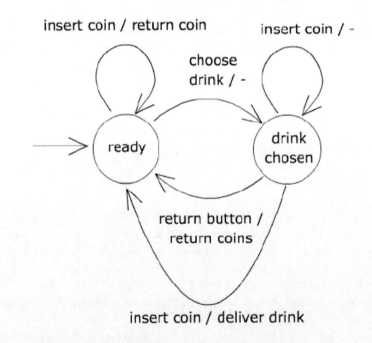

Figure 3. Nondeterministic automaton modeling a vending machine.

Figure 3 shows the state transition diagram of a nondeterministic finite state automaton. It distinguishes only between two states, in which the vending machine behaves fundamentally differently. In the first state called "ready" it does not accept any coins. Any coin that has been inserted is returned. When the customer has chosen a drink, the automaton shows no activity but switches to the second state. Then it takes coins until the required sum is completed and the drink can be delivered or the customer decides to abort the vending process by pressing the return-button. Such state transition diagram is called nondeterministic because state transitions are not defined completely. In the state "drink chosen" the input "insert coin" may trigger the activity "deliver coins" and a transition to state "ready" or the automaton remains in the state "drink chosen". In a real vending machine the transition to state "ready" takes place, when the required amount of money has been collected. But this decision is not modelled by this automaton. It is easier to model this aspect in a different way using a "having-concept". You imagine a container, which stores a number. This value is increased by a certain amount, each time a new coin has been inserted, and it is set to zero, when the automaton switches to state "ready".

The automaton is an abstraction, which focuses on two meaningful states corresponding to certain activities each. Because of the massive abstraction this model is small and intuitive. It might be the starting point of a software development using a programming language. The developer would then define at least three variables, one representing the state and the other representing the value of the collected money and the chosen drink. They are all variables. The programming concepts are identical. But with regard to modelling concepts they represent very different intuitions.

Let me conclude this section with two remarks on the expressive power of finite state automatons. (1) Meaningful states are rich concepts. Several aspects of a system (including input processing and system activities) are wrapped in one Gestalt. This implies a reduction of complexity and cognitive load (Paas et al. 2003). Algorithmic details are ignored on a high level, but can be reconstructed later, when necessary. (2) The basic idea of a state transition diagram is to represent a change of state by a motion from one place to another. The concept of motion seems to be intuitive for human being. The reason might be that we are mobile creatures and a good understanding of space and motion had once been an evolutionary advantage.

State transitions diagrams are used to visualize state-related models in many fields including nontechnical areas (Weigend 2008; 2009b), for instance:

- Transitions between aggregate states (solid, liquid, gaseous)
- Tuckman's model of group dynamics (forming, storming, norming, performing)
- Communication models based on states.

4.3. STATE-ORIENTED THINKING

Holland et al. (1997) observed in university classes on programming that students often believe that an object may have just one attribute. This might indicate a tendency to associate the (one and only) current attribute value to a holistic state. In autumn 2007 I had the opportunity to collect some more specific evidence that in certain contexts people tend to think of states opposed to data-entities stored in containers, when they interpret computer programmes. 26 German high school students (18 female, 8 male) in the age of 16 and 17, who attended a class on informatics in grade 11, were asked to explain the execution of a Scratch program with one variable. They were familiar both with state transition diagrams and variables. The Scratch application contained one sprite visualising a cat reacting to key strokes by thinking or saying something. The following listing shows an abridged version of the scripts (the originally German parts have been translated to English):

```
when green flag clicked
        think "I have nothing to do " for 2 sec
        set activity to 0
stop script
when a-key pressed
        if activity = 0
        set activity to 1
        say "Thank you for the job"
        else
        say "Sorry, I have no time"
stop script
when b-key pressed
        if activity = 1
        say "I have finished the job"
        set activity to 0
stop script
```

The state transition diagram in fig. 4 visualizes the idea of the program. Note that the students did *not* see this diagram.

The students were asked to answer questions like this:

• What happens, when the user clicks the a-key for the first time?

- What happens, when the user clicks the a-key a second time after 5 seconds?

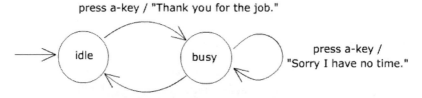

press a-key / "Thank you for the job."

idle   busy   press a-key / "Sorry I have no time."

press b-key / "I have finished the job."

Figure 4. State transition diagram illustrating the idea.

The scripts use one variable named activity. It may contain either 1 or 0, thus indicating, whether the cat is active - and therefore not available for some new job - or not. Therefore this variable is clearly representing a state. But the question is, whether or not the students use the concept of "being in a state" in their verbal explanations. The majority (15 out of 26) used state-related phrases like "The sprite switches to state 1" or "the cat is in state 0" instead of data-related phrases like "The variable activity is set to the value 1" or "activity equals 0". Three students used both state-related and data-related phrases, but 12 persons described the Scratch application exclusively as an automaton moving from state to state.

5. ACTOR MODELS IN PROGRAM VISUALIZATIONS

In the imperative programming paradigm a computer program is considered as a sequence of commands, which have to be executed to achieve a goal. It is assumed that there is only *one* active entity (usually called "the computer"), which does all the work. In this monoactive model, programming means to tell the computer what to do. Especially in the very early days of informatics the monoactive model was very popular. But since computer programs got more and more complex, nowadays people often think of several actors when they try to understand or explain the semantics of program code. In many cases algorithmic ideas are described like theatrical plays. The running program is considered as a system of interacting and cooperating actors. Protagonists are data, names, objects or functions.

5.1. DATA

The idea of "in place"- sorting algorithms is that items (data) in an array change places. Verbal or visual descriptions of this kind of algorithms often use the notion of moving data and ignore the existence of a controlling entity in order to keep the model simple. Moving data entities are also assumed in dataflow diagrams, but the controlling is done mostly by a system of "tracks", on which data are transported from one functional block to the next.

5.2. NAMES

A name identifies a data entity and makes it accessible but does not (in contrast to a literal like 123) represent data by itself. Sometimes data processing activities are visualized in a way that a label, pin, a pointer or some other entity representing a name is moving from one data entity to another. In this case data are static entities and names are actors.

5.3. OBJECTS

Sajaniemi (2002) identified some typical roles that variables can play in programs. For example a "most-wanted-holder" is a variable that contains the intermediately best value - with respect to a goal - , that has been found yet during an iteration. Assigning a role to a variable means allocating activity. The program is considered as a play with collaborating actors.

Consider the following Python program, which computes the sum of some integers that are stored in a list:

```
s = [1, 3, 2, 1, 0, 3]
sum = 0
for i in s:
    sum += i
```

The role of the variable sum is to remember the intermediate sum of those numbers, which have already been read during the iteration. This verbal role description already expresses the major algorithmic idea of the program. A drama-like program visualization might show a "summing-up-machine" hopping over a list of numbers (see fig. 5). This entity consists of a sensor for reading data from the list and a small window, displaying the intermediate sum. At the beginning its value is zero. Each time its sensor touches a list item, its value is added. Combining data and activity to one coherent unit is a way of "information chunking", a metacognitive procedure to reduce working memory load.

From the informatical point of view the "summing-up-machine" is an object, consisting of an attribute and a method for adding a number to the actual value of the attribute. Note that the corresponding program is *not* object-oriented and does not explicitly describe an entity like the summing-up-machine. This object is a fantasy element invented to explain the algorithmic idea of the programme. More advanced fantasy agents are used in algorithmic geometry (see for instance Boissonnat & Yvinec 1998). Explanations of sweep algorithms base on the metaphor of a scan line moving in one direction over a two dimensional arrangement of geometrical elements. Each time the scan line touches an element, some computation is done. Implementations of such algorithms do not model explicitly a continuously moving scan line with the ability of detecting points on a plane. Instead they are based upon simple iterations over a sorted collection of geometrical data.

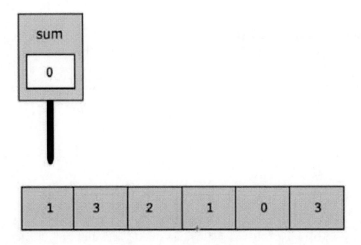

Figure 5. Object as a protagonist in a movie that visualizes a non-object-oriented program. Screenshot from the Python Visual Sandbox.

5.4. FUNCTIONS

According to Lakoff & Núñez (1997, p. 47f) there exist two major "grounding metaphors" for functions in mathematics:

- A function is a machine, taking some objects (from the range, a collection of acceptable Objects) as input making a new objects and returning it.
- A function is a collection of paths from objects in the domain to objects in the range. The operation of the function is the transportation of the domain object to the corresponding range object by an agent.

In the first metaphor the function itself is an active entity whereas in the second it is assumed that there is a superior agent, which is responsible for the execution. The function itself is just a description what to do.

There exists a variety of intuitive models which regard functions as active entities. For example, a function might be seen as a factory consuming data and producing new data or as a tool that changes the state of some (mutable) external object (see section 7.1.).

5.5. ALMIGHTY CONTROL – MONOACTIVE MODELS

Some dynamic models of program execution imply a superior entity which "arbitrarily" change or rearrange other entities. This entity is the one and only actor, all other entities are passive. An example is the visualization of the evaluation of an arithmetic term by successive replacements. First you see a complex term. Then successively parts are replaced or deleted.

(2+1)*4
(3)*4
3*4
12

In Lakoff's arithmetical metaphors for each domain there is a "mathematical agent" being the origin of all activities. In the metaphor "Arithmetic is collecting objects" the mathematical agent is the actor that moves objects. Visualizing the operation 2 + 3 it might rearrange two apples and three apples to a collection of five apples (Lakoff & Núñez 1997, p. 33).

5.6. ALLOCATION OF ACTIVITY IN VISUAL MODELS OF OBJECT ORIENTED PROGRAMS

Multiactive thinking and dramatic interpretation of program code have been cultivated and formalized in Object Oriented Programming. According to this paradigm objects listen to messages and react by performing operations on encapsulated data. Only objects - and nothing else - are origins of activity. But, do people actually use this metaphoric framework when comprehending object oriented programs? Or do they (also) use different concepts?

Consider the following class definition (Python). It models a container, which is containing a certain volume of some substance (attribute content) up to a maximum volume (attribute max). It can be filled (a volume is added), and emptied completely (content is set to zero).

```python
class Container (object):

    def __init__(self, max):
        self.max = max
        self.content = 0

    def fill (self, volume):
        self.content += volume
        if self.content > self.max:
            self.content = self.max # overflow

    def empty (self):
        volume = self.content
        self.content = 0
        return volume
```

In workshops on intuition and programming (Weigend 2007) I asked 23 persons (one university student, one teacher and 21 high school students), who were experienced in object oriented programming, to judge animations that were supposed to visualize the following three statements:

```python
bottle = Container (0.7)
bottle.fill(0.4)
bottle.empty()
```

For each line of code the participants watched a couple of animations, most of them correct or acceptable and some totally wrong. In all movies the Container-object bottle is represented in a naturalistic way by a picture of an antique glass carafe. The message is represented by an oval.

In one of the movie clips (see fig. 6) that visualizes the execution of the statement bottle.fill(0.4) the oval (message) floats to the bottle-object and triggers a magical filling of the carafe. You just see the raising surface of red fluid. All activity is allocated to the addressed *object*, which is consistent to the OO paradigm. 21 of the 23 participants accepted this model as appropriate.

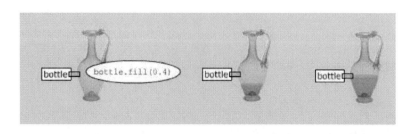

Figure 6. Three screenshots from a movie visualizing the execution of bottle.fill(0.4).

In a different visualization, the filling process is modeled in a more naturalistic but less structurally feasible way (fig. 7). The message goes to some kind of filling device, which fills the carafe with the required amount of fluid. In this case the origin of action is allocated to a fantasy entity (the filling device), which is not mentioned in the program text. Although in the corresponding program the message is clearly addressed to an object named bottle, still 16 out of 23 participants decided that this model is appropriate.

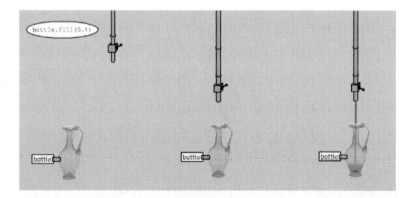

Figure 7. Filling a bottle with a filling device.

One of the animations that model the execution of bottle.empty() adopts an "active message" concept (fig 8.), which is definitively not consistent to the OO paradigm. The message entity has a manipulator that grabs the (passive) object bottle and empties it. Still, 19 out of 23 persons accepted this model.

Figure 8. Message as actor that manipulates a passive object.

The last two described models deviate from the metaphoric framework of the OO paradigm since they do not allocate the origin of activity to the *object* the message is addressed to. But they both display the *result* of the corresponding operation correctly. An example of a totally wrong model for the statement bottle.empty() is shown in fig. 9. When the message (oval) hits the object, both disappear with a yellow flash. In contrast to the semantics of the program, the execution of the statement is interpreted as deletion. Only 4 of the 23 observed players accepted this model, which indicates a pretty good general comprehension of the visual language and the semantics of the presented program code

These results suggest that visual models with entities representing messages and objects might be in general useful for understanding object oriented programs. But details concerning the allocation of activity as prescribed by the OO paradigm seem to be quite unimportant when people imagine the execution of a program. At least in some cases it does not matter, for example, whether the message or the object receiving the message is the origin of activity.

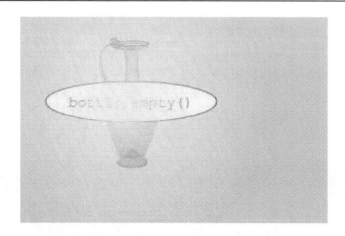

Figure 9. A totally wrong execution model of the statement bottle.empty().

6. NAMING CONCEPTS

Referring to entities using names is an important issue as well in computer programming as in everyday life. Children start to point at things they want to have at the age of one year. A year later they are able to use words like "that" for indicating interesting entities in their environment (....). People refer to an entity by using a name, which is a symbolical representation. Names have two purposes: identification (making something distinguishable from other things) and addressing (make it accessible). In this section I discuss intuitive concepts related to naming data entities within computer programs.

6.1. CONTAINING VERSUS REFERRING

A common intuition for variables in a computer program is the concept of a container for data. The variable may be visualized by a box carrying a label with the name of the variable. Inside the box is a note with something written on it representing the value (data). In this model an assignment like a = 3 is interpreted in this way: A note with number 3 moves to the box and replaces the former content, which is destroyed or removed. The container including its label is used to identify and to access the currently stored entity.

An alternative intuition does not require a container but interprets an assignment as naming an object. I call this reference model, since the name is a reference to an object. In the above example the name a is bound to the number 3. You can visualize the assignment like this: An arrow is drawn from the letter a to the number 3 or a sticky note with an a is attached to a card with the number 3 written on it.

These concepts have some influence on algorithmic thinking. The container model focuses on the name of an object. The labeled container is a persistent entity but its content (data) is volatile and may be replaced from time to time. In contrast, in the reference model the object is the persistent entity. Its name can be changed from time to time. This implies that an object must already exist before it can get a name. It also might happen that it does not get an explicit name at all and remains anonymous.

Another difference appears, when two names are involved. Consider these two lines of Python code:

```
a = 3
b = a
```

How to visualize the execution of the second line? Using the container model a new box labeled with the letter b appears. A copy of the content of box a – a card with number 3 – moves into the new box (fig. 10 left picture). At the end we have two boxes with different labels and two identical data entities.

The second picture of fig. 10 shows a screenshot from a visualization adopting a reference model. It is very simple. A card with number 3 which is already labeled with the letter a gets a second label (name). At the end we have one data entity labeled with two different names.

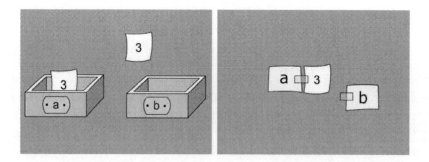

Figure 10. Screenshots from two different animations visualizing an assignment.

Even young kids seem to be quite familiar with both container and reference models, even when they do not know anything about computer programming. In winter 2008/9 I performed a pencil-and-paper exercise – called "Random Park" – with 149 third and fourth graders in German elementary schools (average age 9.2 years). The students had to draw a picture of a park according to given instructions written. Additionally they got a "data sheet" (fig. 11), which they had to use whle executing the algorithm. The instructions deployed a variety of naming techniques including containers, labels and pointers. In some steps the children had to choose a number and place it on the data sheet in an appropriate way. In other steps they had to find an item on the data sheet, using a name.

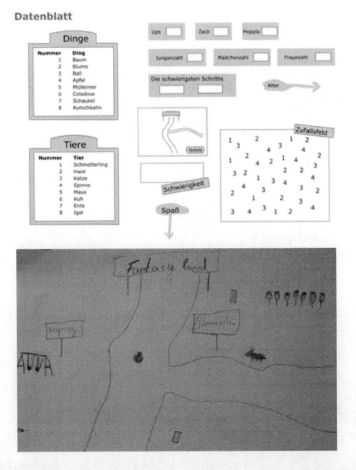

Figure 11.   In the activity "Random Park" children draw a park following given instructions and using a "data sheet" (left picture). The picture on the right hand side shows a result (Weigend 2009a 2009d).

Table 2 shows some instructions and the number students, who were able to execute them correctly. These results suggest that children of that age already understand very well naming techniques using container and reference concepts. However, the instructions did not include changing data. Additionally most of the children were able to use indirect references to data that are constructed from the name of a list and an index (steps 14 and 16).

Table 2.   Some results from the exercise "Random Park".
It was made in Winter 2008/9 by 149 students (average age 9.2 years)
in German primary schools (Weigend 2009a)

Instruction	Correct solutions (n = 149)
Step 7: Ask a girl to tell you a random number between 5 and 9. This number is called *girl-number* (Mädchenzahl). Write this number at an appropriate spot on the data sheet.	146
Step 12: Calculate *ups + zack*. The result is called *hoppla*. Write this number at the correct spot on the data sheet.	142
Step 13: Write your age at the correct spot on the data sheet.	137
Step 14: Draw the thing with number *question-number* (Fragezahl) at the right side of Main Lane.	105
Step 16: Draw the animal number *hoppla* above Flower Lane.	99

6.2. APPARITION MODELS

In case of immutable objects like numbers it is unproblematic to interpret an assignment like b = a as copying data from container a to container b. But things get difficult when mutable objects like lists are involved. Consider this Python program:

```
s = [1, 1, 1]
t = s
s[0] = 5
print t
```

The output on screen is [5, 1, 1] and not [1, 1, 1]. In the second line the one and only list gets second name. That means s refers to the same list as t. This list has been changed in the third line. But it is still the same object. In line 4 this changed list is written on screen.

70 students had to judge four different animations visualizing the execution of the first three lines of this program.

1. The first animation shows an inappropriate model. The list s is represented by a long box labeled with s. It has three compartments each containing a card displaying number 1. A second box with three empty compartments appears. It is labeled with the letter t. From each card in box s a copy is made and goes into the corresponding compartment in box t. Thus we have two boxes labeled s and t with identical content. Box t is a copy of box s. Visualizing the execution of line 3 the number in the first compartment of box s is replaced by 5. Box t remains unchanged. In this case the print statement should write the list [1, 1, 1] on screen, which is not the case. Thus this model is wrong.

2. The second animation resembles the first one. There is only one difference: In both boxes the numbers in the first compartments are replaced by 5 (fig. 12). In this model the box t is not an independent entity. It is not a copy in the usual sense. The boxes are two apparitions of the same entity. Whatever happens to one of them also happens in a magical way to the other. This model is appropriate, since box t represents the list [5, 1, 1].

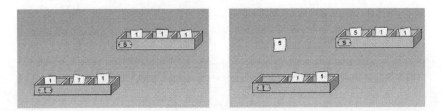

Figure 12. Two screenshots from a visualization adopting an "apparition concept".

3. (3) The third animation again represents the list s by a box with compartments. But the assignment t = s is visualized in a different way. There is no copying. Instead, a second label with the letter t is attached to the box. At the end there is just one box labeled with two names.

4. (4) The fourth model adopts a pointer concept in a very consistent way. List s is a board with a sequence of three pointers pointing to one card with number 1. The two names s and t are also modelled by

pointers referring to the board. After a few seconds the first pointer on the board moves to a card with the number 5.

The students had to answer the following questions:

- Which model would you use to explain the program to someone else?
- Which model do you remember best?
- Which model do you think of, when you imagine the execution of the program?

Table 4 displays the answers given by 70 students from computer science classes in different German high schools (56 male 14 female, average age 17.0 years). The majority chose the apparition model for explaining the program, although models 3 and 4 (adopting a reference intuition) were appropriate as well but were definitively simpler. They consisted of less visual elements and less activity.

Table 4. Choices of different models visualizing list processing. Findings from workshops in 2005 and 2006. Participants were 70 students from computer science classes in Germany (56 male 14 female, average age 17.0 years)

n = 70	Wrong model	Apparitions	Second label	Pointers
Explain	15	40	11	4
Remember	12	23	16	19
Imagine	10	34	17	9
Sum	37	97	44	32

In science theory the apparition model (model 2) may be called an exhaustion of the container model. In this context exhaustion means this: When a scientist makes observations that contradict a hypothesis she or he does not dismiss it at once (and looks for a better model) but tries to "exhaust" it by using additional assumptions in order to explain the contradicting facts with the original hypothesis (Dingler 1913). A well known example in the history of science is the exhaustion of the Phlogiston theory by the German alchemist Hans Georg Stahl (Ströker 1967). At the beginning of the 18th century Stahl believed that a burning substance releases a "fire substance", which he called Phlogiston. According to his theory all inflammable substances contain Phlogiston. When he observed that the product of a burning process is heavier than the burning material, he assumed that Phlogiston must have a negative weight, thus exhausting the Phlogiston hypothesis.

The findings suggest that many people tend to stick to the container/copying intuition to such extend that they exhaust it (assuming several apparitions of an entity), when observing facts that do not fit.

6.3. EXPLICIT AND IMPLICIT NAMES

Names can be explicit or implicit. *Explicit* names are verbal expressions that can be said and written down (Mom, E, sqrt(2), person_1, passenger_list[0]).

Implicit names are gesture-like. They can only be understood taking the context into account. Imagine a customer standing in a bakery and pointing with her finger to some pastry. In this context the gesture is a name for an item she wants to buy. A pin on a map might indicate a certain place, for example a town you already have visited. With a text marker you can identify an important phrase on a page and provide easy access to it.

Implicit names are useful for visualizing algorithmic ideas. They can help to keep a model simple and make it easier to understand. Consider a Python program that sorts a list of four numbers according to the straight selection sort algorithm.

```
s = [10, 4, 1, 3]
for i in range(len(s) - 1):
    for j in range(i+1, len(s)):
        if s[i] > s[j]:            #1
            s[i], s[j] = s[j], s[i]
```

There are two nested for-loops using the variables i and j, which get successively values out of the intervals [0, 1, ... length(s) - 2] resp. [i+1, ... length(s) - 1]. In line #1 the two elements s[i] and s[j] are compared. If the first is larger, they exchange their positions in the list. In case you are not familiar with this algorithm, table 5 might be of help. It displays a tracing of a program run.

Figure 13 shows screenshots from two different Flash-movies that visualize the execution of this program. In both movies the list is represented by a box with compartments containing cards with numbers written on them. The sorting is done through successive swapping of cards.

The first movie shows separated entities for the indices i and j. The visualization was designed as proposed by Sajaniemi (2002). In the movie you can see all possible values of i and j on stripes, which is supposed to clarify their roles as "steppers".

Table 5. Tracing of a sorting program

i	j	s[i]	s[j]	List s after execution of statement #1
0	1	10	4	[4, 10, 1, 3]
0	2	4	1	[1, 10, 4, 3]
0	3	1	3	[1, 10, 4, 3]
1	2	10	4	[1, 4, 10, 3]
1	3	4	3	[1, 3, 10, 4]
2	3	10	4	[1, 3, 4, 10]

The second movie uses implicit names (gestures) to identify the two elements s[i] and s[j] which are going to be compared and eventually swapped: The two cards representing these elements are lifted a little bit out of their compartments (fig. 13 right picture). During the sorting process the first part of the list $[s_0, ..., s_{i-1}]$ is not changed any more, since it is already sorted. In the animation this part is covered and "protected" by a glass box labeled "ok". This box is getting bigger and bigger until it covers the whole container. Note that this aspect of the algorithm is not explicated in the program text.

The connection to i and j in the program can be reconstructed by considering the indices which are written on the box. Additionally one can take into account that i is always the index next to the right hand end of the glass box.

These two Flash movies belong to a collection of four different animations, which have been shown to 16 students (average age 18 years, 3 female, 13 male, 1 university student, 15 high school students). Nine out of them decided they would use the second model with implicit names of list elements to explain the Python program to someone else, and only two chose the first model (Weigend 2007).

What is the advantage of the second model? The marking of two list elements by pulling them out of their compartments focuses the attention to the algorithmic idea. Empirical findings in multimedia instruction research indicate that integrated presentation of information (for instance text fragments integrated in a diagram) - instead of splitting it - facilitates understanding since this reduces the necessary cognitive load (Ayres & Sweller 2005). In contrast, it requires a mental integration of three different visible sources (i, j and the box) to understand the first visualization.

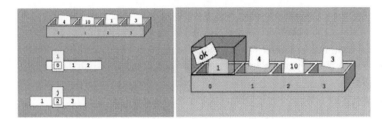

Figure 13. Two visualizations of the straight selection sorting algorithm.

6.4. DIRECT AND INDIRECT NAMES

Explicit (verbal) names can be direct or indirect. A direct name is a name in the most usual sense. It is just a word or a letter, which is connected to an entity in some way. A direct name of an entity can – for instance – be visualized by a sticky note attached to the entity. A direct name is monolithic and can be chosen arbitrarily.

In contrast, an indirect name is constructed from other names. The phrase "my brother's eldest daughter" can be considered as an indirect name, identifying a person (without introducing a new word). In the context of computer programs formal constructions with arrays, dictionaries or aggregate objects are indirect names. For example the term passenger_list[0] is a name for the first item of the sequence passenger_list (Python). A function call can be considered as an (indirect) name for the object the function returns. In mathematical calculations it is common to write √2 to indicate the square root of the number two instead of an explicit literal like 1.4142... (which would be just an approximation). The string √2 is interpreted as a name (identifier) of a numerical object and not as a request to calculate the square root.

6.4.1. Referring to Objects within a Complex Structure

It is quite obvious that it is possible to construct really complex names. But those are difficult to understand and they are not really useful for problem solving mainly because of limitations of the phonological loop (Baddeley).

Working memory load can be reduced by introducing direct names. In a computer program processing complex object structures an assignment like

a = object1.object2.a

enables the programmer (and a reader of the program text) to use the very short name "a" for problem solving (or program comprehension) instead of the long indirect name "object1.object2.a". Thus introducing direct names can be considered as a metacognitive technique to reduce working memory load. It is not only relevant in computer programming but in all areas of information processing whenever referring to entities is involved.

In summer 2009 I performed workshops with students in a German Comprehensive school (grade 9 at the end of the term), in order to get some findings on how people with no explicit computer science education verbalize references to entities. The workshops were entitled "Mission to Mars", since they were embedded in a little story related to our red neighbor planet. Each workshop consisted of four phases:

Phase 1: The students got a picture of a fictive power plant on Mars and instructions (written in everyday language) referring to ten parts of its three-dimensional structure (see table 6). They had to identify entities by writing numbers on the picture. According to the cover story these parts got malfunctions and had to be replaced by a robot. The instructions of phase 1 demonstrated some naming techniques: Explicit names (A, X, corner pyramid) were introduced referring to certain entities within the structure. These names especially facilitated path-like references. For instance the name "corner pyramid" was defined once and used several times as starting point in descriptions of paths to different entities. Some instructions contained the phrase "put your finger on ..." thus using an implicit name for an entity. This technique should help to keep track of a path because it reduces working memory load. When you have put your finger on a thing you need not to remember it.

Phase 2: In phase 2 the students got a picture showing a completely different structure, representing a fictive factory on Mars (see fig. 14 right picture). Six parts got numbers from 1 to 6. The students had to write instructions to identify these parts. There were eight different versions of the task and they were distributed in a way that within a group of students sitting together at one table each task was unique.

Phase 3: Each student exchanged his or her algorithm with someone who had got a different task and who was sitting at a different table in the class room. Then everybody tried to execute the instructions she or he had got from a classmate using the same picture, but without numbers.

Phase 4: The pairs, who had exchanged algorithms, came together and discussed the results.

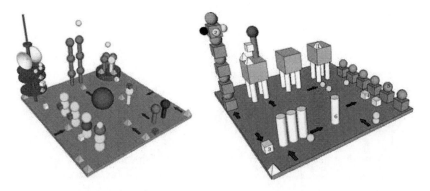

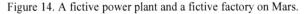

Figure 14. A fictive power plant and a fictive factory on Mars.

The results of phase 1 and 2 were collected and evaluated later in order to get answers to two general questions:

- Did the students understand the naming and referring techniques used in the given algorithm of phase 1?
- Which of the techniques presented in phase 1 did they adapt and adopt for their own instructions?

Apparently the students had no problems to understand the instructions of phase 1. In average they interpreted 95% of the instructions correctly. Nevertheless only a minority made use of direct names themselves. 23 out of 49 students used some kind of naming concept (including implicit naming by pointing with a finger) for individual entities. But just three of them introduced an explicit direct name (like "A" or "corner pyramid"), which they used in several instructions. Another five students used the number of an entity they already had identified to indicate the starting point of a path to a different entity ("Put your finger on part number 3 ...").

What do we learn from this? It seems to be that15 years-old students are not used to invent direct names for things in order to make explanations simpler and more comprehensive. This has to be taught explicitly – for example in computer science lessons.

6.5. NAMES AND ASSOCIATIONS

In imperative programming languages a name is something completely different than the object which is identified by the name. In an assignment statement to the left of the assignment symbol (in most languages like Java, C, Python the equal sign =) stands a name n and to the right an expression indicating an object o. You imagine this expression on the right hand side to be the object itself. After the execution of the assignment, n is a name for o. On the right hand side might a name too. Nevertheless, not this name but the *object* it is referring to, gets the new name n. After the execution of

a = 3
b = a

b is *not* another name of a but another name of the object 3.

Fig. 15 shows two screenshots from animations that visualize the execution of the second statement in an inappropriate way: The name b is attached to the name a. In the first model a chain of labels and in the second a chain of pointers is built.

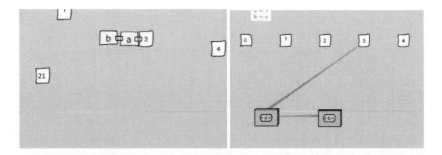

Figure 15. Screenshots from movies visualizing assignments in an inappropriate way.

However, out of 154 students from computer science classes in Germany and Hong Kong 78 accepted the first model (chain of labels) and even 87 accepted the second (chain of pointers).

A possible explanation is that programming novices tend to mix up names and associations. An association is a mental connection between two congenial objects representing some content. In contrast to naming, an association is a symmetrical relation. When a is associated to b, then b is also associated to a. An example is the relation between words with the same meaning. The

German word "Buch" is associated to the English word "book" and vice versa. In contrast to assignments, associations are cumulative. This means two things: First, when building a new association existing associations are not destroyed. The new association is just added. Second, after building a new association between two objects, additional objects might be connected too. For example if "book" is associated to the German word "Buch" and "book" is associated to the French word "livre", then "Buch" is also connected to "livre". This is a difference to assignments attaching names to objects. After the execution of the statements

    a = b
    a = c

there is no connection between b and c and moreover in the second assignment the connection between a and b is destroyed.

7. FUNCTIONS

Functions are an important mechanism to divide a complex program into smaller parts. A function defines some activity which is performed, when the function is called. Thus a program containing function calls is shorter and simpler than a program without functions.

Programming languages usually offer several syntactical constructs for function calls:

- The function may be an independent callable object like in x = sqrt(2).
- A function call may be considered as a message to an object. It is a request to execute one of its methods. Example: x=calculator.sqrt(2).
- A function may be a static method of a class which can be called by a message to the class (instead of an instance of the class) like in x=Math.sqrt(2).
- A function call can be represented by an operator symbol within an arithmetic term, like in x = a + b. Note, that the operator + can be overloaded. Depending on the types the objects a and b belong to, different functions might be called, including user defined functions.

7.1. FACTORY VERSUS TOOL

A function can be visualized by a factory, represented by a box, which takes a number through a hole on one side and outputs the result on the other side. Fig 16 shows an example, visualizing the execution of the Java command

Math.sqrt(2). The factory model fits to the intuition that during a program run data entities move from one location to another.

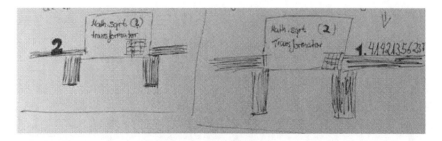

Figure 16. A factory model of a function calculating the square root of a number. Story board designed by a 17 years old high school student (Weigend 2007).

A different type of model, which does not consume data by incorporation, is a tool that moves to some entity and then executes certain modifications. Fig. 17 shows an excerpt from a story board visualizing the execution of the Java statement b = a.toUpperCase().

Figure 17. Visualization designed by a 17 years old high school student (Weigend 2007).

The tool intuition is also adopted in the graphical user interface of many editors. Consider for example the 3D-modeling environment Google SketchUp. Suppose you want to move an entity to a new location. First you select the move-tool by clicking on an icon on the tool bar. The mouse pointer changes its appearance now looking like two crossed double arrows. Then you click on E thus specifying a reference point within the geometry of the entity which is to be moved. When you move the mouse the entity is displayed at the current position of the cursor. When you click the left mouse key again, the entity remains at this position and stays there. In this moment the move-operation has been executed. The state of the entity has changed but not its identity - it is still the same entity. The tool intuition fits to the state intuition for data. While moving an entity on screen by moving the mouse you do not enter explicit data (a spatial vector) but you anticipate its future state.

7.2. DELEGATION OF ACTIVITY

The intuition of functions being actors emphasizes the difference between the definition and the call of a function. The definition of a function is knowledge how to do something. The syntax of the programming language Logo supports this concept: A function definition starts with the key word to followed by a name that should be a verb (e.g. to draw). This suggests that a function definition is some kind of explanation of the meaning of a verb.

The second notion is that of an active entity. When we say "function A calls function B" we assume that A and B are interacting entities. They are in a certain state in each moment of their existence and they can do things. Calling a function is regarded as a social phenomenon. It is seen as delegating a task to another entity, which is able to execute the required operation. This entity might already exist (somewhere out of sight waiting for a call) or is generated at the moment of the call. During a program run there may exist many active entities executing the same procedure but each being in a different states. When actor A calls a new actor B it waits until B has finished its activity and then continues.

Delegation of tasks is a well known phenomenon in everyday life. When the sink in the kitchen is broken we call a plumber to fix it. He is a trained specialist and uses his knowledge to solve the task. Usually there is some hierarchy of responsibility. On top there is some entity responsible for the whole task.

7.3. RECURSIVE FUNCTIONS

Figure 18 is a screenshot from a session with Microworlds EX (LSCI).
The recursive procedure to draw is part of the knowledge of the one and only
one turtle on the field. Within the dramatic framework of Microworlds EX this
knowledge is stored in its backpack. The procedure is an example of end
recursion; the recursive call is the last statement in the body.

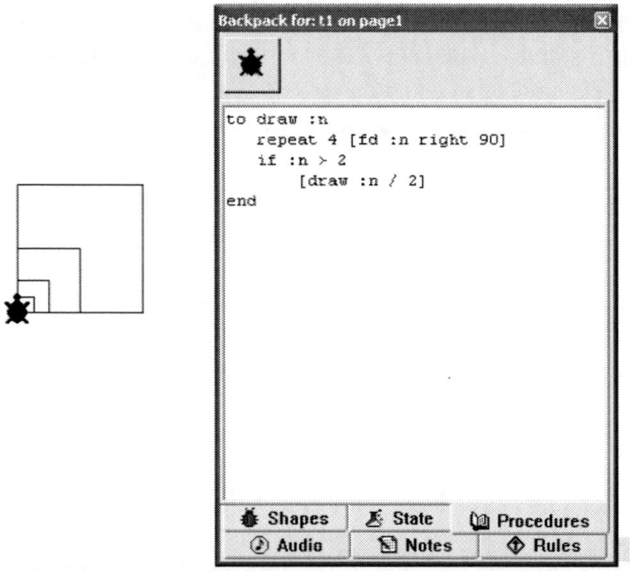

Figure 18. Screenshot from a session with Microworld EX. Working area with turtle t1
and its backpack containing a recursive procedure.

End recursive procedures can efficiently be interpreted using the concept
of repetition. In this case the last statement is read "do the same thing again
but use a smaller number". This concept is easily understood because it
matches with the (tacit) assumption of just one actor.

From everyday life, we are familiar with doing things again but in a
slightly different way. Imagine Tina solving a mathematical problem and
calculating a number. At the end she checks whether the result is correct. If
this is not the case she assumes that she done a mistake and starts again, but
this time she is a bit more careful. Note that the test and the eventual self-
request at the end are part of the solving procedure. But the phrase "do it

again" implies that there is some coherent activity, which already has been completed and thus can be repeated.

The intuitive concept of self-request is appropriate only for end recursive procedures. If the recursive call is not at the end of the procedure body but in the middle (embedded recursion), this model leads to erroneous interpretations. In this case the assumed one and only active entity has to store its actual state. When the activity caused by the recursive call has been finished, this entity restores the state before the call and executes the next statements. But the storage of states is not part of the classical Turtle world and is therefore not visualized in any way. Moreover storing and restoring a state is something quiet unnatural. Since human beings can move in time only in one direction from past to future there is no way to re-gain a state one has been in at some time the past. Therefore there is no direct anthropomorphic representation of such an event.

The delegation model is appropriate to explain recursion. A recursive procedure call can be modeled the same way as any other (non-recursive) procedure call. The calling entity A delegates a task to a new entity B, which just happens to be of the same kind as A. Instead of storing its state the calling entity just waits and remains in the same state until the called entity has finished its work. The concept of waiting is much more familiar and mentally easier to handle than the concept of storing and restoring.

It should be mentioned that the delegation model does not fit to the paradigm of object oriented programming (OOP). In an OOP world objects are the only active entities, they can execute more than one operation (method) and a function call is interpreted as a message to an existing object, which has been generated before.

Chapter 8

8. INTUITIVE MODELING

This section is about cognitive activities taking place during program comprehension. I call the attempt to reconstruct a computer program by intuitive models "intuitive modeling". The main goal of intuitive modeling is gain subjective certainty about structure and functionality of program code. Sometimes it is a silent process of mental elaboration, sometimes it leads to a material result like a story board, a movie or some other kind of visualization.

8.1. IDENTIFYING ENTITIES

One strategy to understand a program is to look for relevant entities that interact in some way. These entities are the protagonists in a drama-like visualization of the program execution. Analyzing an iterative algorithm one might identify the following entities:

- A collection (e.g. a list) of items.
- The "current item", which is to be processed within the loop.
- A function, processing the current item.

Sajaniemi (2002) has developed a system of roles, that variables can take within the mechanics of a program, and has proposed a visualization for each role. Examples are:

- A constants keeps the same value all the time.

- A stepper is a variable, which is initialized with some value and then successively takes values out of a sequence in a predictable way. A stepper might be a counter, which is incremented each time its value is changed, thus stepping through a sequence like 1, 2, 3, ...
- A most-wanted-holder is a variable, containing the best value already found while searching an optimum. For example when you search for the minimum within a collection of items you might need a most-wanted-holder storing the smallest already found item.

A role defines a pattern of behavior and way to interact with other entities within a system of complementary roles. Thus, connecting a variable to a role means assigning it to functionality. In many cases a role is an intuitive concept which already reflects an algorithmic idea. For instance, when you have discovered a certain variable to be a most-wanted-holder you might be on the way to understanding the whole program.

8.2. ABSTRACTION

Abstraction (Latin abstrahere = to remove) means to ignore certain aspects of entities or processes. Automatic systems of program visualization (like Jeliot) fail, because they cannot abstract. They show every detail of the program and cannot distinguish between important and unimportant parts. An intuitive model must be simple. Thus intuitive modeling implies abstraction in the meaning of ignoring the unimportant. This includes:

- Explicit names are omitted.
- Entities are vaguely adumbrated instead of clearly explicated, for example a flash indicating the execution of a function call instead of showing a box taking and returning data entities.
- Data are represented by figurative place holders. A stripe of paper might represent a list in an appropriate way, if just the length of the list is relevant.
- Determinism is replaced by Nondeterminism. For instance, the state transition diagram of an nondeterministic finite state automaton might explain the idea of a complex program.

8.3. GESTALT FORMATION

An intuitive model is a holistic concept (Gestalt). Wrapping the idea of an algorithm in one coherent chunk of information usually includes omitting unimportant details. However, Gestalt formation is not the same as abstraction. Important issues are richness and familiarity. A box with compartments containing lettered cards is a rich and familiar concept representing an array. It is rich because it is connected to a couple of operations like exchanging, rearranging and accessing items at certain positions. These operations are easily recalled, when I see such box, because this is familiar to me. I use boxes that way in my everyday life.

Sometimes fantasy elements are added, which are not part of program that is to explain. The glass box used for illustrating an in-place-sorting algorithm (section 6.3.) is an example. The whole Gestalt is a long box, of which the first part is protected of further change. It represents the main idea of the algorithm but it is not (just) an abstraction since one element (the protecting glass box) is added, which has not been mentioned in the original program.

8.4. ANIMATION

Intuitive models often adopt animism. This is the imagination that things "have a soul" (animus: Latin for "soul") and can act arbitrarily. According to Piaget for children in the preoperational stadium animism is a typical way of thinking (Flavell 1963). An example in program visualization are pieces of paper representing data flying from one place to another, finding their way without external control. Ignoring central control mechanisms simplifies the model. Animism is an essential feature of object oriented programming. According to this paradigm an object manages its data by itself and interacts autonomously with its environment. A special type of animism is anthropomorphism, the interpretation of the world (here: computer programs) in terms of human behavior. Many phrases in informatics technical language embody anthropomorphic models:

• a function accepts arguments and returns something
• a process sleeps, waits for an event or wakes up

8.5. CLUSTERING AND FOCUSING

An intuition is a simplified picture and models formal program code only incompletely. To cope with this limitation intuitive modeling includes creating clusters of different models, each focusing on different aspects.

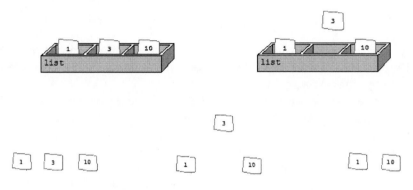

Figure 19. Two different models of a list.

Figure 19 shows two different intuitive models representing a list. The top model (box with compartments) emphasizes that a list is a coherent entity, containing data in separated compartments. Data can be rearranged and exchanged. But the removal of an item is not modeled well. Taking away the content of a compartment does not affect the length of the list. The bottom model is just a linear placement of items. Coherence is represented by vicinity not by a container. In contrast to the box, this intuition models the dynamic length of a list.

8.6. OVERSTRUCTURING – EXPLICATING THE IMPLICIT

An intuitive model is overstructured, when it consists of more details than the program code it is related to. By overstructuring hidden logical implications of atomic program steps can be made visible. It is like using a "logical magnifying glass".

Imagine a movie visualizing the execution of the statement x = 2. You see a box labeled with the letter x containing a piece of paper with number 1 written on it. Another piece of paper with number 2 appears and approaches the box. When it is quite close, it stops. The paper in the box explodes with a bang. The box is empty for a moment and then the piece of paper with number 2 moves into the box.

The execution of the statement on a real computer is just one logical step. There is neither an explicit destruction nor is there a time, when the variable x is "empty". But the destruction of information is an important implication of assignments. And this is visualized by the movie, splitting one atomic step in a sequence of several activities.

8.7. DECORATING AND DRAMATIZING

Decorations are artistic elements of a program visualization that are not directly related to elements of the program. They might constitute comments which are meant to increase the comprehension of the model. Fantasy elements might also be used to build a meaningful story representing a program execution (dramatizing). In visualization exercises with high school students I could observe many decorations. A girl painted numbers with wings flying around from place to place thus visualizing data transfer. Another student invented a dialog between letters (names of variables) explaining a sequence of assignments. In fig. 20 the letter A says: "I am 2. This is my value". The letter B answeres: "My value is greater than yours! You plus 3!"

Figure 20. Dramatizing assignments. Visualization created by a 17 years-old girl in her first year of computer science, grade 11 (Weigend 2007).

8.8. REVERSE MODELING

Computer programs can be considered as models of reality. Reverse modeling is the attempt to create a real life scenario the given program might be an model of. Fig. 21 shows a storyboard visualizing the Java statements

String word;

word = "Hello";

(German words have been translated.) The student, who created this picture, invented a greeting situation. There is a computer, which apparently is able to communicate with humans. And this computer says "Hello" ("Hallo"). The given two lines of code – or similar ones - might occur in a complex program managing human-computer communication. The student possibly tried to find a meaningful context for a per se meaningless program code.

Figure 21. Reverse Modeling. Storyboard designed by a 17-years-old student, first year of computer science, grade 11 (Weigend 2007).

Reverse modeling implies looking for functionality. What is a program used for? According to Pennington (1987) searching for functionality (beside data flows, control structures and states) is one of several cognitive processes that lead to program comprehension.

9. FROM INTUITION TO PROGRAM

Students who are to write a program often have procedural intuitions how to solve the task. Everybody is able to find a book in a library, to sort a deck of playing cards and to search a way from A to B on a street map. Bell, Witten and Fellows (2005) have designed classroom activities on demanding computer science topics (such as text compression, searching algorithms or routing in networks). Even young students (in primary schools) are able to play these games. This suggests that even without special training, children have much intuitive knowledge in the field of informatics. Nevertheless novices often fail writing a program, even when they already know an intuitive solution and know all required elements of a programming language. In this section I am going to discuss some barriers on the way from an anticipatory intuition to correct program code.

9.1. SPLITTING BARRIER

A programmer starts a new project with the confidence that it will be a success. Otherwise she or he would not begin this demanding and time-consuming process. In many cases a programmer has a vision, an anticipatory intuition of the program she or he is going to develop. When you try to implement an intuitive idea you have to destroy its holistic Gestalt first. The Intuition is simple – breaking it up means making it more specific and more complicated. The confidence in the whole idea is gone, when you look at the pieces. So it seems to be plausible to assume some kind of resistance to splitting an intuitive model (splitting barrier).

Spohrer et al. (1989) model the process of program development through goal-plan-trees (GAP-trees). The root of this tree is a plan that represents the original intuitive idea for a solution of the problem. Several subgoals correspond to a plan and all these subgoals must be reached to realize the plan. For each subgoal there exist a couple of different plans representing alternative implementations. But the splitting of a goal into subgoals seems to be a problem. The researchers analysed semantic bugs in 46 novice programmers' first syntactically correct programs. Two observations support the assumption of a splitting barrier. First, 103 out of 549 errors were missing tests of entry data (Spohrer et al. 1989 p. 373). The novice programmers apparently tried to solve a simplified version of the original task first, in order to extend the functionality later. This is basically the strategy of agile software development methodology like Extreme Programming (XP). In XP the developers start with an "architectural spike solution" which is a minimal executable program that models the architecture of the big system that has to be developed. Note, that an architectural spike is not just a *part* of the whole system. It is a simplified *model* of the target product and a preliminary implementation of the anticipatory intuition.

The second observation, which should be mentioned, is that novice programmers tend to merge goals. That means they avoid splitting and use a single plan to achieve several goals in an integrated manner.

9.2. DIFFICULT ANTICIPATORY INTUITIONS

Sometimes an anticipatory intuition is too difficult to implement. Consider this classroom activity: The students are asked to file in front of a wall sorted by height. They do this in some way and then discuss *how* they did it. While solving the problem and discussing the algorithm, an intuition like this might evolve: "Everybody moves to a place in such way that the person on her or his left hand side is not taller (if there is a person)." It is obvious that items can be sorted in that way. The simplicity of this idea is partly achieved by using the concept of parallel processing. The objects to be sorted are supposed to act independently. The intuition describes the behaviour of a single object and ignores the necessity of a central control mechanism. But it is very difficult to implement this idea in a "straight forward" manner. Each number would have to be represented by a separate thread. The programmer would have to develop complex protocols for the communication between the objects taking into account the possibility of deadlocks and infinite loops. This intuitive idea –

though easy to grasp – is not appropriate for (direct) implementation – at least by a novice. You might call it a misleading intuition. It is important to recognize this as early as possible and search for a different approach.

9.3. MISSING CONNECTIONS BETWEEN INTUITIONS AND FORMAL PROGRAM CODE

Tom is able to find a telephone number in a telephone book. He also is familiar with programming concepts like variables, lists, if-statements and loops. Still, he fails, when he has to write a program that finds a specific tuple in a sequence of tuples. He knows for sure what to do but is not able to express this knowledge using the programming language. It might be that some mental connections between intuitive models and corresponding program code are missing. Of cause, it also might be, that the knowledge which enables Tom to find a telephone number is completely procedural, and he is not aware of the underlying algorithm which controls his acting. But since Tom is a rational being, he is able to observe himself, reflect his behaviour and find some kind of description.

To develop a program on the basis of an anticipatory intuition, Tom has to analyse it in depth. Let us take a close look on the cognitive processes taking place during such analysis. A major activity is to look for elements one is able to implement with programming language. A specific point is identifying and naming entities. The problem is that in the intuitive model explicit naming is avoided in order to keep it simple. Imagine Tom searching a telephone number within a list which is written on a piece of paper. Each line contains a pair (name, telephone number). To search for the number of a given person, Tom moves his finger from the top of the list down checking in each line whether or not the string at the beginning of this line is the name he is looking for. When he has found it, he moves his finger to the right and reads the corresponding telephone number. The difficulty is to recognize that pointing with a finger is a way to name an entity. For the line Tom's finger is pointing to, the program must introduce an explicit name (variable) giving access to a tuple (name, telephone number). Going through a list of tuples might be explicated and implemented by a construction like

```
for item in telephone_list:
    do something
```

The telephone number within the tuple item can be accessed by the indirect name item[1]. A programmer needs to know such connections between intuitive gestures and programming concepts. Writing a computer program on the basis of an anticipatory intuition means to explicate implicit features using a programming language. Thus, knowledge about how to visualize program code (intuitive modeling) should be of help on the way in the other direction, when analyzing an intuitive model in order to write a program. Chiu (2001) observed in the field of mathematics that experts could name more different metaphors explaining arithmetic operations they used to solve a problem than novices.

Perkins et al. (1989) observed, that successful problem solvers were able to explain a program line by line. They call this activity "close tracking of code". The researchers also analysed teachers' scaffolding strategies. The most successful cues were those, which focused on close tracking of code ("Explain your program!"). While trying to explain, students detected logical errors by themselves. Whenever people try to tell other persons what they think how a program works, they are forced to externalise internal models of programming concepts.

Knowing these connections between intuition and formal program text seem to be part of computer science expertise.

REFERENCES

Anderson, J. R. (2004). *Cognitive Psychology and Its Implications*. 6th edition. New York: Worth Publishers.

Ayres, P., & Sweller, J. (2005). The Split-Attention Principle in Multimedia Learning. In Richard E. Mayer (Ed.), *The Cambridge Handbook of Multimedia Learning*. Cambridge University Press, pp. 135–146.

Baddeley, A. (1998). Recent Developments in Working Memory. *Current Opinion in Neurobiology,* Vol. 8, Issue 2, April 1998, 234–238.

Baddeley, A. (2003). Working Memory: Looking Back and Looking Forward. *Nature Rewies Neuroscience,* Vol 4 October 2003, 829–839.

Balzert, H. (1999): *Lehrbuch der Objektmodellierung: Analyse und Entwurf.* Heidelberg Berlin: Spektrum Akademischer Verlag.

Beck, K. (1999). *Extreme Programming Explained.* Boston San Francisco New York Toronto Montreal London Munich Paris Madrid Capetown Sydney Tokyo Singapore Mexico City: Addison Wesley.

Bell, T., Witten, I. H., & Fellows, M. (2005). *Computer Science Unplugged.* http://csunplugged.org/

Capurro, R. (1986). *Hermeneutik der Fachinformation.* Freiburg/München: Alber Verlag 1986.

Cooper, J. W. (2003). *C# Design Patterns. A Tutorial.* Boston, MA: Pearson Education.

Chiu, M. M. (2001). Using Metaphors to understand and solve arithmetic problems: Novices and experts working with negative numbers. *Mathematical Thinking and Learning,* 3.3, 93–124.

Dehn, M. J. (2008). *Working Memory and Academic Learning.* Hoboken, New Jersey: John Wiley & Sons.

Dingler, H. (1913). *Die Grundlagen der Naturphilosphie.* Leibzig.

English, L. D. (2004). *Mathematical and Analogical Reasoning of Young Learners.* Mahwah: Lawrence Erlbaum.

Fischbein, E. (1987). *Intuition in Science and Mathematics.* Dordrecht Boston Lancaster Tokio: Reidel.

Fromm, E. (1976). *To have or to be?* New York: Harper and Row.

Gamma, E., Helm, R., Johnson, R., & Vlissides, J. (1995). *Design Patterns: Elements of Resuable Object-Oriented Software.* Reading, MA: Addison Wesley.

Haberlandt, K. (1994). *Cognitive Psychology.* Boston London Toronto Sydney Tokyo, Singapore: Allyn and Bacon.

Jeffries, R. (2001). *What is Extreme Programming?* http://www.xprogramming.com/ xpmag/whatisxp

Krauss, R. M., & Fussell, S.. R. (1991). Perspective-taking in communication: Representations of others' knowledge in reference. *Social Cognition,* 9, 2–24.

Lakoff, G., & Núñez, R. E. (1997). The Metaphorical Structure of Mathematics: Sketching Out Cognitive Foundations for a Mind-Based Mathematics. In L. D. English (Ed.) *Mathematical Reasoning. Analogies, Metaphors, and Images* (pp. 21–92). Mahwah New Jersey, London: Lawrence Erlbaum Associates.

Matthews, D., Lieven, E., & Tomasello, M. (2007). How Toddlers and Preschoolers Learn to Uniquely Identify Referents for Others: A Training Study. *Child Development,* Vol. 78, Issue 6, 1744–1759.

Paas, F., Renkl, A., & Sweller J. (2003). Cognitive Load Theory and Instructional Design: Recent Developments. *Educational Psychologist,* 38 (1), 1–4.

Perkins, D. N., Hancock, C., Hobbs, R., & Martin, F. (1989). Conditions of learning in novice programmers. In E. Soloway, & J. C. Spohrer (Eds.) *Studying the novice programmer.* Hilsdale: Lawrence Erlbaum Associates.

Paivio, A. (1971). Imagery and language. In S. J. Seagl (Ed.) *Imagery: Current cognitive approaches* (pp. 7–32). New York: Holt, Rinehardt & Winston.

Paivio, A. (1986) *Mental representations – a dual coding approach.* Oxford: Oxford University Press.

Riehle, D., & Züllighoven, H. (1996). Understanding and Using Patterns in Software Development. In K. Lieberherr & R. Zicari (Eds.) *Theory and Practice of Object Systems,* Vol. 2 (1), 3–13.

Smith, J. P., diSessa, A. A., & Roschelle, J. (1993). Misconceptions Reconceived: A Constructivist Analysis of Knowledge in Transition. *Journal of the Learning Sciences,* Vol. 3 Nr. 2.

Spohrer, J. C., Soloway, E., & Pope, E. (1989). A Goal/Plan Analysis of Buggy Pascal Programs. In E. Soloway, & J. C. Spohrer (Eds.): *Studying the novice programmer* (pp. 355–399). Hilsdale: Lawrence Erlbaum Associates.

Ströker, Elisabeth (1967). *Denkwege der Chemie.* Freiburg, München.

Weigend, M. (2005). Intuitive Modelle in der Informatik. In S. Friedrich (Ed.) *Unterrichtskonzepte für informatische Bildung: INFOS 2005 Proceedings* (pp. 275–284). Bonn: GI.

Weigend, M. (2006). Experimental Programming. In D. Watson & D. Benzie (Eds.): *IFIP WG 3.1, 3.3 & 3.5 Joint Conference, Alesund,* Norway 2006 Proceedings.

Weigend, M. (2006a). Design of web-based educational games for informatics classes – some insights from workshops with the Python Visual Sandbox. In A. Schwill (Ed.) *GML – Grundfragen multimedialer Lehre.* Potsdam 14. – 15.3.2006.

Weigend, M. (2006b). From Intuition to Programme. In R.T. Mittermeir (Ed.) *Informatics Education – The Bridge between Using and Understanding Computers. ISSEP 2006 Vilnius, Litauen Proceedings* (pp. 117–126). Berlin Heidelberg: Springer.

Weigend, M.(2007). *Intuitive Modelle der Informatik [Intuitive Models in Computer Science.* Potsdam: Universitätsverlag.

Weigend, M. (2007a). Origins of action: protagonists in drama-like interpretations of computer programmes. *IMCT 2007* Northeastern University Boston, USA.

Weigend, M. (2007b). Logo Nanoworlds. *EuroLogo 2007* Bratislava Proceedings.

Weigend, M. (2007c). Analog denken – analog programmieren. *INFOS 2007 Universität Siegen, Germany, Proceedings* (Poster).

Weigend, M. (2008). To Have or to Be? Possessing Data versus Being in a State – Two Different Intuitive Concepts Used in Informatics. In R.T. Mittermeir, & M.M. Syslo (Eds.) *ISSEP 2008 Torun, Poland* (pp.151–160). LNCS 5090, Berlin: Springer.

Weigend, M. (2008a). How to Tell a Joke? Modeling Communication in Informatics Classes. In S. Wheeler, S., A. Kassam, & D. Brown (Eds.): *LYICT 2008, Kuala Lumpur, Malaysia.* Proceedings on CD-ROM, IFIP, ISBN: 978-3-901882-29-6.

Weigend, M. (2009). How to Take Care of an Alien? New Multimedia Games
    for Teaching Algorithmic Concepts in Primary Schools. *M-ICTE Lisbon
    Portugal*.
Weigend, M. (2009a). Applying Informatics Knowledge to Create 3D Worlds.
    IFIP WCCE, Bento Goncalvez, Brazil 2009 Proceedings.
Weigend, M. (2009b) State- and Data-Oriented Models in Program
    Visualization. *IFIP WCCE, Bento Goncalvez, Brazil 2009 Proceedings*

INDEX

tracking, 64
training, 61
transfer, 4, 5, 59
transition, 23, 24, 25, 26, 56
transitions, xi, 2, 23, 24
transport, 21, 22
transportation, 29
trees, 62
triggers, 23, 31
turtle, 52

U

UML, 5, 16
uncertainty, 10

V

validation, 9
values, 7, 41, 42, 56
variables, 9, 11, 12, 21, 24, 25, 28, 35,
    41, 55, 59, 63

vector, 51
visible, 43, 58
vision, 14, 61
visual images, 5
visualization, 5, 28, 30, 32, 36, 39, 42,
    43, 55, 56, 57, 59

W

walking, 1
water, 10
web, 67
web-based, 67
winter, 36
working memory, 4, 6, 28, 44
writing, 44, 61

Y

yield, 12